$8.00

D1467729

THE PITCHERS

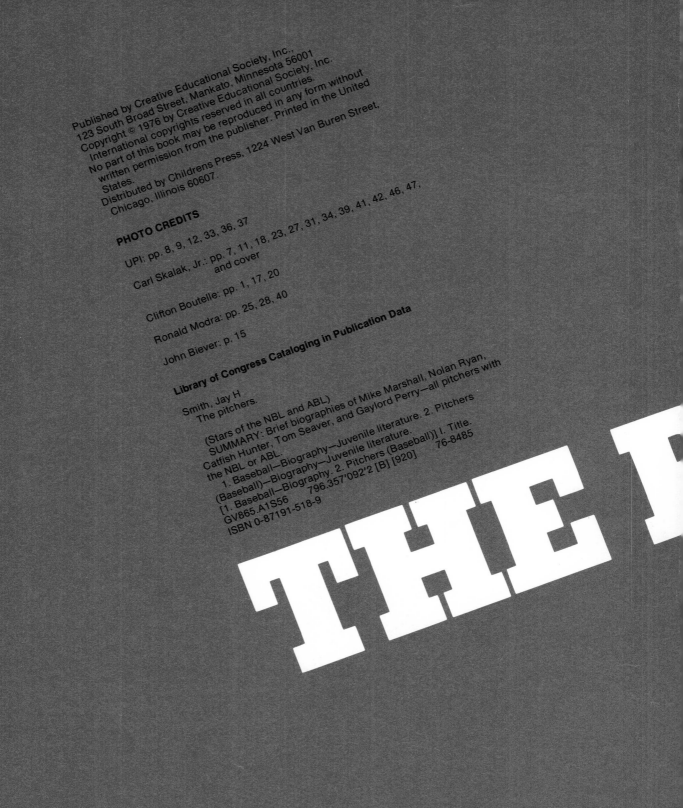

Published by Creative Educational Society, Inc.,
123 South Broad Street, Mankato, Minnesota 56001
Copyright © 1976 by Creative Educational Society, Inc.
International copyrights reserved in all countries.
No part of this book may be reproduced in any form without
written permission from the publisher. Printed in the United
States.
Distributed by Childrens Press, 1224 West Van Buren Street,
Chicago, Illinois 60607.

PHOTO CREDITS

UPI: pp. 8, 9, 12, 33, 36, 37

Carl Skalak, Jr.: pp. 7, 11, 18, 23, 27, 31, 34, 39, 41, 42, 46, 47,
        and cover

Clifton Boutelle: pp. 1, 17, 20

Ronald Modra: pp. 25, 28, 40

John Biever: p. 15

Library of Congress Cataloging in Publication Data

Smith, Jay H
    The pitchers.

(Stars of the NBL and ABL)
    SUMMARY: Brief biographies of Mike Marshall, Nolan Ryan,
Catfish Hunter, Tom Seaver, and Gaylord Perry—all pitchers with
the NBL or ABL.
    1. Baseball—Biography—Juvenile literature. 2. Pitchers
(Baseball)—Biography—Juvenile literature.
[1. Baseball—Biography. 2. Pitchers (Baseball)] I. Title.
GV865.A1S56   796.357'092'2 [B] [920]   76-8485
ISBN 0-87191-518-9

THE P

STARS OF THE NL & AL PITCHERS

by Jay H. Smith

CREATIVE EDUCATION/
CHILDRENS PRESS

MIKE MARSHALL 6

NOLAN RYAN 14

THE PITCHERS

CATFISH HUNTER
22
TOM SEAVER
30
GAYLORD PERRY
38

MIKE MARSHALL

The group of young Los Angeles Dodger fans eagerly surrounded their idol. But their happy expressions faded to ones of keen disappointment when Mike Marshall refused to sign their autograph books.

Baseball's most famous relief pitcher paused to explain. He would be glad to sign, he told them, if their books also included the signatures of people "really meaningful" in their lives. Like their teachers, for example.

Not surprisingly, none of the boys could show him such signatures. As he left the crowd of bewildered youngsters, Marshall hoped they would eventually understand what he had said.

Mike Marshall is a man of strong beliefs and opinions. He questions many of the values that exist in the sports world.

"As an athlete," Marshall once told a reporter, "I am no one to be idolized." In his opinion, professional ballplayers are just not as special as many people seem to think. It worries him that hero worship plays such a big role in the American sports scene. Marshall feels that this is a distortion of values.

Mike Marshall doesn't think of himself as a hero. It would be better, he feels, if the fans didn't think of him as one, either. The important thing in sports, he believes, is the quality of an athlete's play and not the person himself.

True to his philosophy, Marshall refuses to take advantage of his famous name off the field. He won't attend sports banquets where athletes often receive big fees for making speeches. He does no TV commercials, promotes no products.

Marshall doesn't want to be treated like a product either. He rarely gives interviews and hardly ever talks with fans.

"Just watching me perform," he has said, "does not give someone the right to steal my time off the field and thrust himself upon me."

Then he continued, "A lot of people get upset because I won't talk to them in a public place where I'm eating. That doesn't bother me at all. There's something sadly missing in these people."

Marshall's motives are not always understood. Trying to clear up one misunderstanding, he said, "They say I don't like kids; but I think that by refusing to sign autographs, I am giving the strongest demonstration that I really do like them. I am looking beyond . . . to what is truly valuable in life."

Dodger Pitcher Andy Messersmith hoped to straighten out some of the misconceptions about his teammate. "Mike is a very blunt, very honest person," Messersmith told a sportswriter. "Some people can't handle that. I know a lot of people think he's some kind of bad dude, but really he's a considerate and warm person."

Some baseball fans might not like Marshall's ideas, but they certainly do appreciate his excellent pitching. In 1974 he had the best year of his career. Leading the Dodgers to the National League pennant, Marshall made a record-breaking 106 appearances in relief. During one incredible period, he pitched in 13 games in a row.

His 15 victories, 21 saves, and 2.42 earned-run average (ERA) made him an easy winner of the annual award *The Sporting News* presents to the National League's best relief pitcher.

But Marshall earned an even more impressive honor. He was voted the coveted Cy Young Memorial Award as the very best of *all* pitchers in the league. It was the only time in baseball history that this award has gone to a reliever.

Good relief pitchers generally make many appearances during a season, but no reliever has ever pitched as often as Marshall.

Many people feel that the Dodger ace is able to do what he does simply because he's stronger and more talented than any other reliever around. Marshall disagrees.

He claims that his effectiveness is due to hard work and study. Marshall is no ordinary student of the game. He holds a Ph.D. degree in physiological psychology from Michigan State University.

During his many years at Michigan State, Marshall analyzed all aspects of pitching scien-

tifically. He studied kinesiology — a branch of science concerned with how the mechanics of the human body affect movement.

Marshall learned many things about how the body works. He discovered the right muscles to use for each type of pitch he throws. It is because of this knowledge, he says, that his pitching arm never gets sore.

Marshall's favorite weapon is the screwball, a very difficult pitch to throw. It requires a severe twist of both the elbow and the wrist which can easily result in serious injury to the arm or shoulder. Often young pitchers who don't have Marshall's knowledge are forbidden by their coaches to throw it.

Another result of Marshall's studies was a new approach to conditioning. Managers generally make their players run wind-sprints to keep in shape. Marshall believes long-distance running is more effective. Although weight lifting is usually frowned upon by baseball experts, Marshall feels that such training, if properly controlled, can be beneficial.

Like all pitchers, Marshall keeps a ''book'' on all the hitters in the league; but he does more than that. He makes notes on every pitch he throws during the entire year, listing its type and how his opponent handled it.

Although Marshall is always well prepared mentally and physically when he comes in from the bullpen to pitch, there is another quality equally important to his success. He has the emotional stability to handle the intense pressures relief pitchers are subject to.

This is one of the reasons Los Angeles Manager Walt Alston never hesitates to bring Marshall into a game. ''An effective relief pitcher,'' says Alston, ''has to have ice water in his veins. Mike does.''

All of Marshall's special attributes make him a winning pitcher; but for him, that's not the point of the game.

''Our whole society,'' he has said, ''is deluged with the concept that winning is all that's

important. But all that's really important is that the individual does the best he can.

"Victory," he added, "does not elate me, nor does defeat depress me. The only victory for me is in the quality of the competition, not in the final score."

Some of Marshall's Los Angeles teammates are beginning to understand his point of view. "People here," he says characteristically, "are slowly discovering that there *is* life after baseball."

During most of Marshall's stormy career, such understanding was rare. In 1973 when he was a member of the Montreal Expos, Marshall's outspokenness angered many sportswriters and several teammates as well. However, being unpopular didn't affect his performance at all. He appeared in 92 games for the Expos and was credited with 14 victories and 31 saves.

At the end of that season a Montreal brewery, the Expos' TV sponsor, presented an award to the team's Most Valuable Player. No one was surprised when Mike Marshall's name was announced, and nobody should have been very surprised when he rejected the honor.

Later he sent a letter to the president of the brewery, indicating why he turned down the award and the $10,000 automobile that went along with it.

"I can't imagine players on the same team competing for this kind of award," Marshall wrote.

The next season Marshall was no longer wearing a Montreal uniform. He had been traded to the Dodgers.

Mike Marshall loves to play baseball, but he says it is only a hobby. His main interest is education, and he has been a part-time instructor at Michigan State.

It is likely that the 33-year-old pitcher will retire from baseball before long and become a full-time professor. When that day comes, baseball will have lost one of its most original thinkers.

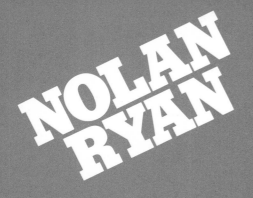

NOLAN RYAN

No one in the history of baseball ever threw as hard and as fast as Nolan Ryan. When the California Angel pitcher has complete control of his blazing fastball and explosive curve, no other player today can create as much excitement.

Ryan lacks the game-after-game consistency of pitchers like Catfish Hunter and Tom Seaver; but at his best, he is an unequalled artist who can make beautiful things happen.

He was in top form against the Detroit Tigers on July 15, 1973. The Tigers were as capable of appreciating beauty as any other group of people, but they found it very difficult to enjoy Ryan's artistry that day.

The Detroit batters had much in common during that game; all of them shared a feeling of extreme frustration. Sometimes they didn't appear to feel anything at all. They stood numb with their bats on their shoulders, watching helplessly as the ball whizzed by at slightly more than 100 miles per hour.

After seeing Ryan strike out 12 of the first 14 men he faced, Tiger Norm Cash decided that something had to be done to relieve the tension. So he came up to bat with a huge paddle almost as wide as home plate. The umpire, of course, tossed the paddle out of the game.

The joke helped the Tigers to relax, but it didn't do them any good against Ryan. At the end of eight innings, Detroit still had not managed to get a hit.

Norm Cash was scheduled to bat again in the ninth. This time he came out of the dugout carrying a piano leg wrapped in tape. Under the circumstances the umpire probably felt a bit of sympathy for Cash and the Tigers, but he had to enforce the rules. The piano leg was also thrown out.

14

16

The game was quickly over after that. Ryan had struck out 17 on the way to his second no-hit game of 1973. Two months earlier he had performed the same feat against the Kansas City Royals. At 26, the young righthander had become only the fifth man in the history of the major leagues to pitch two no-hitters in the same season.

As exciting as those two performances had been, neither could quite match the drama of Ryan's last start of the year against the Minnesota Twins.

Nolan had 367 strikeouts so far that season. Only the great Sandy Koufax, with 382, had ever struck out more in a single campaign. But time was running out for Ryan, and the 16 strikeouts he needed to break the record wouldn't come easily against the hard-hitting Twins.

Ryan was wild that night, constantly struggling to find the strike zone. To make matters worse, the Minnesota batters were pounding the ball hard on occasion.

The grace of his best performances was gone, but Nolan made up for it with raw power and courage.

At the end of nine innings the score was tied, 4-4. Between walks and base hits, Ryan had sandwiched 15 strikeouts. He had tied Koufax's record, and it looked as if one more would be easy enough to get.

But in the ninth Ryan had suffered a severe cramp in his leg, which hindered his delivery. Now he wouldn't be able to throw his fastball at top speed.

Ryan held Minnesota scoreless in the top of the tenth, but he didn't strike anybody out. The Angels almost ended the game in their half of the inning; but luckily for Nolan, they couldn't quite score the winning run.

Visibly tired and in pain, Ryan came out to pitch in the eleventh. He knew he wouldn't be able to continue much longer.

Angel fans booed as the first two Twins hit the ball for easy outs. Then Rich Reese came to

the plate. After getting two strikes on Reese, Nolan reared back and put everything he had left into the next pitch. When the Minnesota slugger swung and missed, a mightly roar thundered in Nolan's ears.

He had his record; and when the Angels scored in the bottom of the inning, Nolan had his twenty-first victory of the year as well.

Ryan threw another no-hitter in 1974, the third of his career. He won 22 games for the Angels. He also set another record, becoming the only man ever to strike out over 300 batters three years in a row.

Ryan's fourth career no-hitter came early in 1975 against the Baltimore Orioles.

"A guy like Ryan," said Baltimore's Dave Duncan after the game, "doesn't get you out, he embarrasses you. There are times when you feel you've won some sort of victory just hitting the ball."

Off to his best start ever, Ryan won 10 of his first 13 games. But serious arm trouble hindered him from then on. Nolan, who had started out so well, finished the season with a 14-12 record. Toward the end of the year he was trying to find the perfect combination of rhythm and timing he had displayed earlier.

"I just want to go out there and regain my form," he said, "and then go home and get ready for next season."

If Ryan's arm is strong again in 1976, he could become the first pitcher ever to throw five no-hitters. Sandy Koufax, who also has four to his credit, predicts Ryan will pitch 10 during his career.

Nolan declined to comment on possible no-hit games, but he was certain he'd be better than ever when the new season rolled around.

Such strong belief in himself and his ability is typical of Nolan Ryan these days. But it was not always so. His first four years in the major leagues were filled with doubt and depression.

From 1968 through 1971, Ryan played for the New York Mets. The Mets had several fine pitchers on their roster, and almost all of them were more consistent than Nolan. Consequently, he didn't get much of a chance to pitch.

Infrequent opportunities to play slowed his development. His famous rising fastball was as unpredictable as it was amazing. He had not yet mastered the sinking curveball that makes him so brilliant today, and his change-up was practically nonexistent then.

He had other problems as well. He was constantly troubled by blistered fingers on his pitching hand. Besides, Nolan, a shy youngster from a very small town in Texas, found it extremely difficult to adjust to life in New York City.

After four years of waiting for the promising

young pitcher to succeed, the Mets' management finally grew disenchanted with Nolan. At the end of the 1971 season, they traded him to the California Angels.

It was exactly what Ryan needed. With the Angels, who had a weak pitching staff at that time, he would be able to pitch regularly.

Ryan developed rapidly. Before the 1972 season was over, he had already become one of the top pitchers in the American League. Before long, he was the Angels' team leader as well.

"In his own low-keyed way, Nolan's taken charge," says California Manager Dick Williams. "He's so thoughtful and responsible, I'd like my son to be like him."

Now that he is a superstar, Nolan finds that he has less free time than he once had. There are banquets to attend and television shows to appear on. While he endures the demands made upon him with grace and warmth, Nolan would prefer to spend a quiet afternoon with his wife Ruth and young son Reid.

Every year during the off-season, the Ryans leave the hectic world of baseball far behind. They return to their home in tiny Alvin, Texas, where both Nolan and Ruth were born and grew up.

Fame and wealth don't appear to have changed the life-style or values of the Ryans. They live well but simply. The quiet, uncomplicated country life they have chosen to maintain seems to suit them.

Nolan appreciates the financial security baseball has given him, but he tries to keep such things in perspective. "The thought of being paid so much is staggering," he once said. "I can't believe it. It will let us build a home, which we never would have done. It's a chance to achieve some goals.

"But," he added, "it won't change the way we live."

CATFISH HUNTER

In 1974 Jim "Catfish" Hunter won 25 games for the Oakland A's, his fourth straight 20-game season. He received the Cy Young Award as the American League's outstanding pitcher, and he played a key role in his team's third consecutive World Series triumph.

But for some mysterious reason, A's Owner Charlie Finley was unhappy with his star pitcher. He refused to pay part of Hunter's $100,000 contract.

Hunter, of course, was not at all pleased by this. He made his feelings known to league officials. A special committee was then set up to arbitrate the rather strange case.

On December 16, 1974, a decision was reached in favor of Hunter. Charlie Finley not only lost the case, he also lost Hunter. The committee ruled that since Finley's actions were illegal, he had no further rights to Hunter's services.

This meant that Hunter was now a free agent — free to play for any other team he chose. With the exception of the San Francisco Giants, every other major-league ball club tried to land the Catfish, but the New York Yankees came up with just the right bait.

Hunter signed a five-year Yankee contract worth over three million dollars, making him the highest paid baseball player in history.

That offer wasn't even the highest. The San Diego Padres, one of the National League's worst teams, were willing to pay more; but Hunter turned them down. He wanted to stay in the American League where he knew the hitters, and he preferred to play for a pennant contender. The Yankees' offer seemed perfect in every way.

News of the fabulous contract made headlines all across the United States. Even people

who took no interest in baseball were talking about Hunter. His fortune fascinated them. His name intrigued them.

Until the Yankees made him a multi-millionaire, Hunter had never really received a great deal of public acclaim. Now much of what he does and says is highly publicized. A very private person, Hunter would prefer not to be the center of so much attention. Nevertheless, he handles his sudden fame with patience, good will, and an engaging sense of humor.

Still, it embarrasses him when people show so much interest in his life. He doesn't think it's really all that special.

James Augustus Hunter was born on April 8, 1946, at Hertford, a small farming community in North Carolina. For the first six or seven years of his life he was known simply as Jimmy. Then one day he ran away from home.

"When my folks found me," Hunter once told an interviewer, "I was sitting by a stream with a string of catfish next to me. I didn't really want to run away, so I went fishing." From that time on, he was always called Catfish.

Some reports of Hunter's life have read like a fairy tale — the classic rags-to-riches story of a poor, miserable country boy who came to the big city and struck it rich.

The Hunter family certainly wasn't rich, but neither was it poor. Catfish's childhood was happy and uncomplicated. Although he worked hard on the farm, there was always ample time for hunting and fishing and playing sports.

"I wouldn't have changed my boyhood years for anything," Hunter says.

Hunter played several sports in high school, though baseball was always his favorite. But he had no desire to be a pitcher then. Hitting home runs was much more exciting.

But it was his pitching that attracted the most attention. During his high school career Hunter pitched five no-hitters. Big-league scouts flocked to Hertford to see the young righthander in action.

"I remember a game," Hunter said, "when I struck out 29 men in 12 innings. I sort of thought those scouts would be interested in that."

Then Charlie Finley came from Kansas City, where his A's played until he moved them to Oakland in 1968.

"I had never heard of him or the Kansas City A's," Hunter told a reporter, "until one day he pulled into town in a big black limousine with a motorcycle escort. Nothing like that had ever happened in Hertford before. He put his arm around me and started handing out jackets and bats to everybody. The other scouts started thinking he had me all signed up, so they stayed away."

Finley soon found out that it was easier to eliminate the competition than to sign the young pitcher. After lengthy negotiations, he finally agreed to meet Hunter's demand for a $75,000 bonus.

Hunter's first year as a professional was in 1964. But because he had to have foot surgery, he didn't throw a single ball. Baseball rules at that time required major-league teams to keep bonus players on their rosters, so Hunter didn't have the opportunity to get minor-league experience in 1965. Instead, he sat on the Kansas City bench, doing almost nothing for the first half of the season.

But then one of the A's regular starting pitchers was injured, and Hunter was named to replace him. He finished the season with a respectable 8-8 record.

During the next two years, Hunter continued to improve. By 1968 he had established himself as one of the outstanding players on the team. On May 8 of that year, the A's played their first home game in Oakland. Hunter was selected to pitch against the visiting Minnesota Twins.

It was destined to be the most memorable night of his career. When it was over, he had pitched a perfect game. He gave up no hits,

26

walked no one, and there were no Oakland errors.

His happy teammates tried to carry him off the field on their shoulders, but Hunter refused. "I didn't want any more fuss," he said later. "I just wanted to get out of there. I was embarrassed."

Ever since then, he has avoided as much fuss as he possibly could. Hunter's desire to stay out of the limelight has been helped, strangely enough, by his pitching style. There is nothing spectacular about the way he plays. He doesn't have the blinding speed or the beautiful grace that really excite the fans. He creates very few dramatic moments.

All Catfish Hunter does is win games. Pinpoint control, consistency, stamina, and a keen mind are his strongest attributes. But these qualities do not often gain headlines.

Among professionals, however, Hunter is regarded as a pitcher's pitcher, a master of his craft.

Although the Yankees had to pay a fortune to get him, they figured Hunter was worth the price. He was the kind of winner they sorely needed.

During much of the history of baseball, the New York Yankees had dominated the game, always taking great pride in their winning tradition. But since 1964, they had not won a championship of any kind.

Yankee fans were not buying as many tickets as they once did. The team's owners felt that Hunter would eventually lead the team back to the top — and the fans back to the ballpark. No matter what, they knew many people would come simply to see baseball's highest-paid player.

Aware of the Yankees' great tradition, Hunter said, "Just walking into Yankee Stadium sends chills through you."

So much is expected of him that naturally Hunter feels pressure to produce great results. So far, he hasn't let it bother him. Taking the pressure in stride as he has always done, Hunter had another outstanding season in 1975. He won 23 games, tying Jim Palmer of the Baltimore Orioles for the major-league high.

Despite Hunter's fine performance all year long, the Yankees didn't win their division title in 1975. Obviously, one man couldn't solve all their problems.

But many baseball experts have not given up on the Yankees. Some feel that 1976 will be their year. If it is, much of their success is sure to come from the good right arm of Catfish Hunter.

TOM SEAVER

One day during the 1975 season, Ted Simmons of the St. Louis Cardinals was talking to a reporter about the most difficult pitchers to hit. "Tom Seaver's the best around," the Cardinal slugger said.

Many people in baseball agree with Simmons. Others who don't share his opinion are willing to concede that Seaver is the most complete pitcher in the game today. His skillful pitching is a unique combination of power and finesse, knowledge and desire.

Tom Seaver is a proud and confident man. Every time he takes the mound, he believes he can win. The New York Met righthander is not always victorious, of course; but his winning attitude has given him a very impressive record.

In his nine years in the National League, Seaver has won 168 games. Four times he has recorded 20 or more victories in a single season. He has led the league three times both in strikeouts and in earned-run average. His ERA in 1971 was an amazing 1.76.

In each of his last eight seasons, he has struck out over 200 batters. No other pitcher in baseball history ever matched that mark. In 1970 against the San Diego Padres, he tied the major-league single-game strikeout record of 19. In that game, he broke another record, striking out ten men in a row.

Seaver's brilliant performances have earned him numerous honors. He won the Cy Young Award in 1969 and 1973. When the ballots for 1975 are finally tabulated, he could be the winner again.

He was the Rookie of the Year in 1967. In 1969, *Sports Illustrated* magazine selected him Sportsman of the Year. In eight of his nine

30

seasons, Seaver has been named to the National League All-Star squad.

These individual honors have meant a great deal to Seaver. But all of them put together could not equal the thrill of being part of the 1969 Mets team. That was the year the Miracle Mets, as sportswriters called them, amazed and shocked and gladdened the baseball world.

Until 1969, the team had never finished better than next to last. Ever since 1962, their first year in the league, the Mets had been the joke of baseball. With the exception of Seaver and a few others, they had always been a collection of lovable losers.

But in 1969 they could do no wrong. They won their division and took the National League play-offs. Then in the World Series, the Mets upset the powerful Baltimore Orioles. New York fans were almost crazy with joy, and so were the Mets. They had good reason to be. They had achieved great things. For Seaver, a man intensely dedicated to excellence, that was what it was all about.

"Pitching is what makes me happy," Seaver once said. "I've devoted my life to it."

His devotion has already made him a happy man. Still, he is not entirely satisfied with what he has accomplished so far. For Tom Seaver is a perfectionist, and it is his nature to drive himself to ever greater achievement.

"I want to prove I'm the best ever," he has said. He knows it won't be easy to reach that goal, but he has to try. It won't be the first time that the odds were against him.

When he was growing up in Fresno, California, Tom was the youngest of four children in a very athletic and competitive family. Tom's father was once one of the top amateur golfers in America. He had been a member of the 1932 United States Walker Cup Team which defeated the British.

Tom's mother was also an excellent golfer, and his brother and two sisters were natural athletes who later starred for their college teams.

It isn't surprising for a child brought up in such a sports-loving environment to show an interest in athletics at an early age. By the time he was five, Tom had already decided he would be a big-league baseball player one day.

Tom's love of baseball continued to grow. Everything about it excited him. Every year at World Series time he would pretend to be sick. That way, he could stay home and watch the games on TV.

Tom played for four years in the Spartan League which is equivalent to the Little League, but he was never very impressive. He was small, couldn't throw very hard, and displayed little natural athletic ability.

Nevertheless, Tom clung stubbornly to his dream of a major-league career. As time went on, however, he began to worry. At 14 he started to think seriously about his shortcomings as a pitcher. Even if he couldn't do much about his physical limitations, he figured that at least he could try to master the mental aspects of the game.

Tom soon discovered that he had several adjustments to make, and he set out to change his style.

Realizing at last that he couldn't throw the ball past the batters, Tom began to concentrate on keeping them from hitting it solidly. The only way to do this, he learned, was to stop pitching across the middle of the plate. Instead, he would have to aim for the corners.

It became clear to him that everything depended upon his control. Accuracy was just as important as speed. It would be all right now if he didn't get any strikeouts, just so long as he didn't walk anyone.

Tom worked diligently during the next few years, absorbing all he possibly could about the art of pitching. The more he learned, the more he improved.

Even so, his frustrations were far from over. In his junior year in high school, Tom found out that he was still not even good enough to make the school team. He did earn a place on the team when he was a senior; but at season's end, all he could show for his efforts was an unspectacular 5-4 record.

No big-league scouts came to offer him a contract, and no colleges were interested in giving him a scholarship. For the first time in his life, Tom figured it was about time to start thinking of a career in something other than baseball.

During the summer after high school graduation, he grew four inches in height and gained 30 pounds. Tom, who was now six-foot-one and weighed 190 pounds, was sure the additional height and weight would help him throw harder. But he wasn't going to take any chances. He worked out with weights in order to turn those extra pounds into muscle.

The following spring, he was pitching for Fresno City College. After losing his first two games, Tom won 11 in a row. For the very first time, he was beginning to attract attention.

Coaches from the University of California (USC) came to watch Tom play and immediately

offered him a full scholarship. Tom transferred to USC in the fall of 1964. That next spring, he compiled an excellent 10-2 record against the best college teams in the country.

Major-league scouts were interested in him now. Early in 1966, Tom signed with the New York Mets. He was sent to Jacksonville in the International League. There, he gained valuable experience. By 1967, he was ready to move up to the Mets.

National League batters were impressed with Tom's mental maturity and knowledge of pitching, qualities rare in a rookie.

Many young pitchers reach the majors by relying on raw physical ability alone. Then they have to begin to learn what pitching is all about. It often takes them four or five years of hard work and study to reach a high level of effectiveness. Fortunately for Tom, he had been through all of that years before.

Tom Seaver was a star from the beginning of his major-league career. Everything went smoothly for him until 1974. Then a hip injury almost ended his career. Trying to compensate for his bad hip, he altered the rhythm of his motion and placed excessive strain on his arm. He finished the year with a mediocre 11-11 record.

When spring training opened in 1975, Seaver worried that he might not be able to pitch as well as he once did. Typically, he came back better than ever. He won 22 games in 1975, and he had added an excellent change-up to his fine assortment of pitches.

Now he is looking ahead to 1976 and beyond. Only 32, he should have many good seasons left in his arm. Nothing would suit Tom Seaver better. For baseball is his life, his way of expressing himself.

"As a pitcher, I feel i'm creating something," he says. "Pitching itself is not enjoyable while you're doing it. Pitching is work. I don't enjoy it until I can stand back and look at what I've created. That is something."

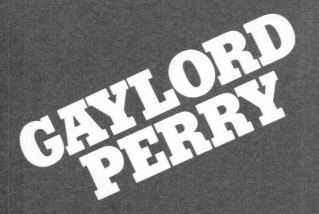

GAYLORD PERRY

It was early in 1974, and snow still blanketed the ground in many cities. Spring training was still a month away, but some fans were already thinking about baseball. They eagerly searched the sports pages for news of their favorite players and teams.

Some of them were reading Gaylord Perry's newly-published autobiography, a book as witty and controversial as the famous pitcher himself.

Perry had a confession to make. For the first time publicly, he admitted having thrown an illegal pitch throughout most of his long career. The pitch in question was the spitball, sometimes called the greaseball. Some fans were amused by what they read in Gaylord's book, others were shocked.

To people in baseball, however, the news came as no surprise at all. Almost every player, manager, owner, and umpire in the game was well aware of Perry's spitball. Some of them, in fact, had known about it as early as 1964, the year Perrry first started to throw the devastating pitch.

Because it was old news, most baseball men didn't find Perry's confession very exciting reading. But something else in his book really did interest them. He had written that he wouldn't be using his "greaser" anymore.

Players who had been tricked repeatedly by the almost unhittable outlaw pitch were especially relieved, but none of them believed that Perry's decision was prompted by sympathy for their sagging batting averages. The truth was, he had no choice in the matter. A tough new spitball rule had just been passed which would make it impossible for him to get away with it any longer.

The new rule, of course, had not been aimed at Perry alone. One out of every four major-

league pitchers also threw the spitball; but because no one used it as often and as effectively as Perry, the new rule became popularly known as ''Gaylord's Law.''

Some players wondered how Gaylord's Law would affect Gaylord himself. Many of them were convinced that he couldn't win without the spitball. Perry, however, didn't appear worried. He had developed so many other effective pitches, he said, that giving up one of them wouldn't hurt him at all. Perry looked forward to proving just that in the 1974 season.

The umpires were also looking ahead to 1974. The new rule would make their difficult jobs a bit easier. Although the spitball had been banned for over 50 years, the officials had never found a way of stopping it. The old rules were simply impossible to enforce.

But all of that was to change. The new rule eliminated the need for evidence. Now if an umpire even suspected a spitball was being thrown, he could toss the pitcher out of the game.

When the season began, many people were keeping a careful, questioning eye on Gaylord Perry. If he had really reformed, could he still win? If he hadn't changed at all, would the sly old fox be able to get away with it?

Perry jumped off to the best start of his career. No other pitcher in the majors was throwing so well or winning so often. Naturally, some people began to get a little suspicious.

Perry said he owed his success to a new and absolutely dry pitch, a forkball which he had recently developed. But this wasn't enough to quiet the doubters. They were quick to point out the curious resemblance between the movements of the forkball and the spitball.

In order to prove his innocence, Perry arranged a demonstration for senior umpires. He convinced them that the forkball is really a different pitch after all. The umpires could see that it is thrown slower and with an entirely different grip. Although it does dip and dance, it lacks the sharp, dramatic dive characteristic of the spitball.

The skeptics were still not convinced, however. All his demonstration proved, they said, was that Perry did throw a legal forkball and *not* that he had stopped throwing the spitball. Perry, they claimed, was simply using the forkball as a decoy for his old illegal pitch.

Perry didn't appreciate this kind of talk, but it didn't surprise him. He knew it would be difficult to live down his reputation.

His angriest critics continued their protests throughout the 1974 season. Although they never managed to prove anything against him, they kept their suspicions just the same.

For others, however, the controversy was over. Perry had shown them two important

43

things. Not only had he abandoned the spitball, he had proved he could win without it. When the season was over, Perry's record for the weak-hitting Cleveland Indians was 21-13. His ERA of 2.52 was even more impressive.

Perry was traded in 1975 to the Texas Rangers, for whom he posted an 18-17 record. Those victories gave him a career total of 216 wins, a figure any pitcher would be proud to have.

In addition to the lively debate about his spitball, Perry has had many other problems to overcome in his 13-year major-league career. There were years when his usually excellent fastball was often uncontrollable. There were seasons in which he was very inconsistent. But Perry, a fierce competitor, always managed to reestablish himself as one of baseball's greatest pitchers.

With the San Francisco Giants in 1966, his record was 21-8. In 1968, he pitched a no-hitter for the Giants over the St. Louis Cardinals. A 23-13 record followed in 1970.

In 1972, his first year with the Cleveland Indians, he won 24 and lost 16. An ERA of 1.92 earned him the Cy Young Award as the American League's top pitcher that season.

At 37, Perry is nearing the end of his career. But as long as he can pitch effectively, he wants to remain in the game. Even his severest critics hope that Perry stays around a long time. They realize that he is one of the most colorful men in baseball. Although they never liked his spitball, they couldn't help liking Gaylord himself. They respect his talent and admire his spirit.

Many of them were honest enough to admit that they themselves had also bent the rules a bit from time to time. They could understand Gaylord's strange logic when he defended the use of a pitch he knew to be against the rules.

"I never said I cheated," Perry had told a sportswriter. "I just said I was throwing something everybody else was."

44

Gaylord was exaggerating quite a bit, of course. About three-fourths of the major pitchers had never used the pitch. Some of them, no doubt, had avoided it because it was just too difficult to master. Others, however, chose to abide by the rules, even if they thought the spitball should be legalized.

One of these men is Gaylord's older brother Jim, a pitcher for the Oakland A's. Jim's career has been almost as outstanding, though certainly not as controversial, as Gaylord's. During his 16 years in the majors, he has won over 200 games. In 1970, when he was with the Minnesota Twins, Jim was the recipient of the Cy Young Award.

Gaylord and Jim grew up at Farm Life, a group of farms not far from Williamston, North Carolina. Their father, Evan, taught them all he could about the game.

Evan Perry had been an outstanding amateur baseball player in his younger days. He was offered a minor-league contract then, but he had to turn it down. He was needed on the farm.

When they were growing up, Jim and Gaylord played baseball as often as possible. After their chores around the farm were done, they would run out to a meadow and practice throwing and hitting until nightfall. Evan Perry soon saw that they were very talented youngsters.

He made up his mind to give them every opportunity to play. "There was a lot of work to do myself," he once said, "and I did it. I let them go.

"It's a real thrill to see the boys in the big leagues," he continued. "It's something I'd like to have done."

Gaylord and Jim have gone far, achieving fame and fortune along the way; but they have never forgotten their humble beginnings or what their father did for them.

Today, Gaylord owns the farm his father worked as a sharecropper. Gaylord Perry is glad that his success has given his father a chance to take things a little easier at last.

THE PITCHERS
STARS OF THE NL & AL

THE INFIELDERS
STARS OF THE NL & AL

THE CATCHERS
STARS OF THE NL & AL

THE HITTERS
STARS OF THE NL & AL

THE MANAGERS